W9-BQY-590

The world's best reading golf

The Anatomy of Greatness

Lessons from the Best Golf Swings in History

Brandel Chamblee

Foreword by
Tom Watson

CLASSICS
OF GOLF
The world's best reading golf books.

New York   London   Toronto   Sydney   New Dehli

SIMON & SCHUSTER
1230 Avenue of the Americas
New York, NY 10010

CLASSICS OF GOLF
120 Research Drive
Stratford, CT 06615

First Classics of Golf/Simon & Schuster hardcover edition April 2016

SIMON & SCHUSTER and colophon are registered trademarks of Simon & Schuster, Inc.

CLASSICS OF GOLF is a registered trademark.

For information about special discounts for bulk purchases, please contact Simon & Schuster Special Sales at 1-866-506-1949 or mail to: business@simonandschuster.com.

The Simon & Schuster Speakers Bureau can bring authors to your live event. For more information or to book an event, contact the Simon & Schuster Speakers Bureau at 1-800-248-3049 or www.simonandschuster.com.

Interior design by Sally Bancroft, Bancroft Graphics

Illustrations by Gairen Tembreull, Albatross Studios

Manufactured in the United States of America

10 9 8 7 6 5 4 3 2 1

Library of Congress Cataloging-in-Publication Data is available.

ISBN 978-1-5011-3301-5
ISBN 978-1-5011-3302-2 (ebook)

To my parents, Harrel and Sandy,

who have always been there and are always ready to help.

Contents

Foreword

Some of my life's most cherished times were spent in the same room with Byron Nelson listening to him tell stories about his life and the game we both truly loved. One of these wonderful stories involved a reporter who came to him in the locker room one day and told him what Ben Hogan had said about Byron's practice habits: "If Nelson practiced harder he would become a better player" was the gist of his needle. Bryon needled back: "Go tell Hogan that I have already learned how to swing the golf club!"

Indeed, Byron didn't practice as much as Ben did. Nobody did, as Hogan was legendary for his extensive practice sessions in which he "dug it [his secret] out of the dirt." The point of this is the difference in their two different psyches. Byron of knowing his golf swing and trusting that he knew it and of Hogan's who was rarely satisfied with his swing and who was always searching for the secret, possibly reaching as closely to the Holy Grail of the perfect swing (for him) as anyone ever.

Both players were arguably among the greatest ever in our sport but each had markedly different golf swings. They approached practicing differently but shared a similar trust in the mechanics of their own swings. In fact Byron told me that for his entire career he made only one major change to his swing that really mattered. It was in the early 1930s when steel shafted clubs were introduced, greatly reducing the clubhead torque, or twisting, of the shaft/clubhead at impact compared to the hickory shafts in use up to that time.

Instead of having to more forcefully rotate, or release, the hands through impact to help square the clubface as you had to do with the flimsier hickory-shafted clubs, the stiffer steel-shafted clubs allowed him to keep the clubface square to the aiming line a lot longer in the impact zone. Byron accentuated this by driving both legs toward the target on the downswing more than any other top pro at that time. He called this his "rocking chair" motion, which resulted in a pronounced dip of his head on the downswing and through impact. It's a fact that high speed motion camera studies of his swing confirmed that Byron kept his clubface square to his aiming line longer than any of the top pros of his era, and this is why Bryon hit the ball so consistently straight.

As far as golf instruction goes, there have been countless swing comparisons of the Great Triumvirate of Hogan, Nelson, and Sam Snead as there have likewise been of Nicklaus, Woods, and McIlroy. Golf professionals, instructors, and analysts of all different persuasions dissect the golf swing, trying to define the specifics of why each swing works or doesn't work. This is where many times we tip-hungry golfers get confused, as the conversations become too minutely technical for the golfer to understand and/or perform in the one-plus second it takes to complete a golf swing.

What Brandel describes in this book is what he sees as certain historical, and proven, fundamentals of instruction that in this day and age have been overlooked as the key elements to build a consistent golf swing. Of course any instruction starts with what connects you with the club: one's grip. This is how I start any discussion of the golf swing: by making the observation whether or not the golfer's grip is fundamentally sound—meaning, will the hands deliver a square clubface to impact repeatedly under pressure? Brandel describes the grip in terms that should be remembered by all golfers.

The fundamentals of the grip, setup, and swing can never be taken for granted. A case in point was Jack Nicklaus. At the end of his 1979 season, during a rare low point of poor play in his career, he called up his lifelong teacher Jack Grout and said, "Let's start off from scratch, starting with the grip and setup, then with the movement of the golf club. Let's first make certain my foundation is solid." This is how the greatest player in the game approached his problematic game…and it worked. Jack won both the U.S. Open and the PGA Championship the following year.

In this book, Brandel, after sorting through today's golf instruction and its many conflicting methodologies, describes what has historically been proven to work in the teaching of golf's fundamentals, and from which we can build a consistent golf swing. May your journey to find your best golf swing stop here.

—Tom Watson

Introduction

I'm often asked where I would send my children for a golf lesson if they were just beginning to play. Certainly there are many knowledgeable men and women golf professionals who can set a child on a path to a lifetime of enjoyment playing the game, but when it's your own children and their education—be it in golf or anything else—a parent wants only the best. For colleges, the choice is often Harvard. But where is the Harvard of golf?

While I can point to several teachers who have been very successful at the highest levels and more than a few players who seemed to know what their peers didn't, in their differences, both of ideas and technique, where is the glitter and where is the glue?

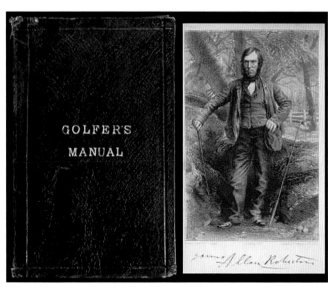

Written in 1857, the first book on golf instruction.

From the first instruction book, Henry Brougham Farnie's *The Golfer's Manual* (1857), to the last instruction book or article you read, millions of words have been parsed about the little more than a second it takes the average Tour pro to make a swing. And every year new technologies are advanced that allow for a deeper understanding of that fraction of a second when the clubhead meets the ball. Yet there have never been more theories, argument, and debate about the golf swing.

Perhaps golf's greatest teacher, Alex Morrison.

In *Bobby Jones on Golf*, Jones states that:

"In examining and comparing the methods of various players it is always necessary to be aware of the difference between mannerisms and fundamentals."

Very often, it is the player's mannerisms or idiosyncrasies that divert our attention from what one great player has in common with another, and to this point Jones continues:

"When we set side by side the playing methods of the best golfers, we always find that the basic movements and their orderly sequence are the same within a very narrow range."

This principle is the central theme of this book: There is one best way to learn this game and to play it, and it can be found in the commonalities of the greatest players of all time. These commonalities are the Harvard of golf.

No great player ever swung more upright than Jack Nicklaus or flatter than Ben Hogan, and yet these two players have much in common. Besides their records, both are linked to the ideas of an instructor from the Los Angeles area in the first half of the twentieth century by the name of Alex Morrison.

Morrison was one of the first to use high-speed photographs to analyze golf swings, and according to Grantland Rice, he "exerted more influence on the game and the method of playing it than any individual in the memory of man." Morrison was sought after by the Hollywood stars of that era and his prolific thoughts on the swing changed the games of hundreds of thousands of golfers and were advocated by none other than Bobby Jones. And Jones's own swing, with only one exception (he didn't kick his right knee in at address), was a perfect distillation of Morrison's thoughts.

One of Morrison's students, Henry Picard, had Ben Hogan's ear.

Henry Picard taught Jack Grout, who went on to teach Jack Nicklaus.

Alex Morrison taught Henry Picard, who won twenty-six times on the PGA Tour, including two majors, but is perhaps more famous for helping Ben Hogan. Hogan never won an event, let alone a major, until he heeded the advice of Picard, passed down to him from Morrison.

Alex Morrison also taught Jack Grout, who had little success playing the Tour but was unequaled as a teacher. Grout passed Morrison's theories on to a young Jack Nicklaus.

So in Morrison you had one man whose ideas were endorsed by Bobby Jones and handed down to Ben Hogan and Jack Nicklaus—any one of which could be argued to be the greatest player of all time.

Byron Nelson, conversely, learned the game by trial and error and then won more events in succession than anyone before or since. Although his record of eleven wins in a row is sometimes saddled with the caveat that those wins came in the last year of World War II, his scoring average of 68.33 for that year wasn't bested until Tiger Woods averaged 68.17 in 2000. And Nelson's 1945 Sunday scoring average of 67.45 still stands unequaled.

Byron Nelson taught scores of touring professionals, most notably Ken Venturi and Tom Watson. Venturi, in turn, taught John Cook and many others. Tom Watson, meanwhile, never won a major until after he was mentored by Byron, and then he went on to win eight.

Whether passed on through explanation or imitation, or discovered through great toil, the commonalities of the greatest players look like a family tree linking one generation of stars to the next.

In every facet of this game, from the grip to the finish, the best players have been materially linked by these commonalities, which have separated the good from the great.

It is easily within the grasp of every player who picks up a club to improve his or her game in a very short period of time by being aware of and incorporating the timeless principals of the swings of those players whose swings have held us spellbound.

The records of Jack Nicklaus inspired Tiger Woods.

How to Use This Book

Golf is unique in sport for its difficulties. The many tedious little things, done or not done, can make a world of difference in one's golf game. Were this not true, we might see batters laboring in the batter's box over their grip on the bat and their alignment and stance. We might also see the best in professional tennis constantly rehearsing their serving motions. We might see all other sorts of athletes in between their respective periods of play, rehearsing movements that long ago became involuntary to them. But we don't. Such is the case in golf, though, that the technical fretting of professional and amateur alike remind me of an old man watching his life savings on a park bench, vigilant to a fault lest we lose it all in a moment.

I think this difficulty lies in the nature of our sport. We are tasked with hitting a stationary object. There is nothing reactionary—contrary to most other sports—about golf. The ball just sits there, which gives us all too much time to think, and in thinking we tend to freeze.

With this in mind, I offer as a caveat to the reader that the tendency in this game is to become so caught up in a specific change one is making, that the attention to that detail robs one of the fluidity that is so important.

In each of the chapters that you are about to read, you will likely come across something new to you—something that might, at least initially, be tedious to change. And in making those changes it is very easy to become rigid and forget that each step, from the time one takes hold of the club until the ball is in the air, is meant to flow right into the next one.

It is also very easy—and I speak with some authority on this subject, having read hundreds of instructional books—to rush from chapter to chapter in an effort to put the whole puzzle together as fast as one can. *Take your time with this book and savor the nuances.* Each chapter builds on the next one; each chapter contains timeless principles that, once mastered by the greats in this game, became intuitive, and as such were more easily demonstrated by them than articulated.

With this is mind, I took great pains to find the right photographs for the various points of this book, in hopes that any ambiguity of the text will be alleviated by the clarity and commonality of the examples.

The men and women in this book spent thousands upon thousands of hours perfecting the moves you are about to read. So if you find yourself struggling, take solace that the best also struggled. Their struggles, however, have led to the discoveries and commonalities in this book, so take your time, and this may well be the last instruction book you will need.

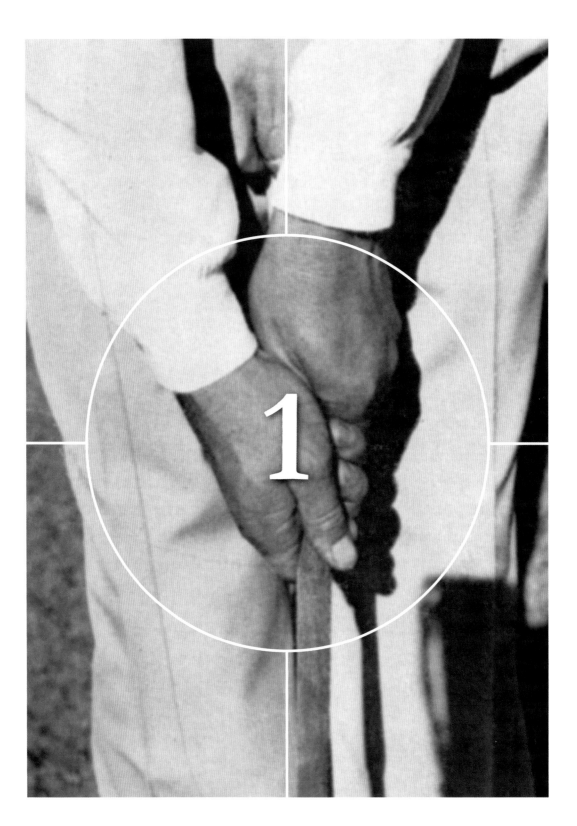

The Grip

The single most important aspect of the golf swing happens well before impact—the gripping of the golf club. The hands are the only connection to the club, and nothing contributes more to the overall look of the swing and—more important—the quality of shots played than how they are placed. This is just as true at the highest levels of this game as it is for the beginner.

Among professionals there is a deep respect for grips. To a pro, a proper grip is not only considered functional, it's regarded almost as a work of art. And while not every grip looks alike, the variety is mostly in how players link their hands together. Beyond the differences of interlocking, overlapping, or ten-finger style, the grips of most of the best players of all time have much in common.

Among amateurs there is often some confusion and much error when it comes to placing their hands on the club. I believe much of the problem is rooted in the most popular instruction book ever written.

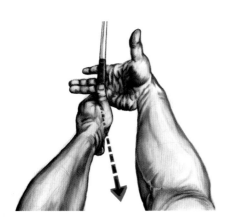

Hogan's weak preference.

On page 26 of *Five Lessons: The Modern Fundamentals of Golf,* Ben Hogan states that, when placing your left hand on the club, the V formed by the marriage of the index finger and the thumb (for a right-handed golfer) should point to the right eye. On page 28 he states that the V formed by the index finger and thumb of the right hand should point to the chin. In professional golf-speak, this is known as a weak grip. Hogan's was one of the most beautiful the game has ever seen.

It was beautiful because Hogan could curl his right thumb backward from the joint as he pushed the joint into the side of the club and because this gave him the ability to push the inside of his thumb hard against his index finger. This connection gave a definite line, or V, which Hogan used as a guidepost for the grip, and he believed that V should be pointed at his chin. It was beautiful because he crooked his right index finger, which he called a trigger finger, back just enough to where he could push the top joint into the side of the grip and apply pressure and this cohesiveness, between index finger and thumb, gave his grip an almost unmatched symmetry.

The beautiful symmetry of Hogan's grip.

No one had ever described the placing of the hands on the club in such a manner, but many amateurs took it as gospel because of what came to be known as the "Hogan mystique."

Hands with V's pointing to the right shoulder.

Ben Hogan was and still is one of the most compelling characters in the game of golf. That he was able to overcome such obstacles as a traumatic childhood (his father committed suicide when Ben was nine years old), diminutive size, and a near-fatal auto accident made him a heroic figure. His relentless, dig-it-out-of-the-dirt work ethic was universally admired. The Hogan mystique created a cult-like obsession with every facet of Hogan's game, including his grip.

The problem was that Hogan's grip didn't work for everyone. It worked for him, in that it corrected the tendency to hit violent hooks that nearly drove him out of the game prematurely. But most amateurs have the opposite tendency—they slice the ball—and Hogan's grip only exacerbates that fault.

Thanks to modern technology that allows us to measure, with great accuracy, what happens at every point in the swing, we know that at impact the hands are roughly five inches in front of where they were at address. Dr. Ralph Mann and Fred Griffin pointed this out over two decades ago based upon their computer-generated model of hundreds of professional golfers. In their book, *Swing Like a Pro,* they presented that a golfer should have a stronger grip, and

Hogan's necessary compensations.

that the V's of both hands, and in particular the right hand, should be turned to the right. This is a considerably stronger position than Hogan's.

With Hogan's grip, the pushing of the hands forward at impact tends to open the clubface. Hogan corrected this by bowing his left wrist and supinating, or turning counterclockwise, both his left forearm and wrist.

As beautiful as Ben's grip was, it was unique to him. The vast majority of great players have used a much stronger grip, and most amateurs should, too. A stronger grip is the grip of choice—the commonality among the best in the game—and the easiest path to improvement.

The Left Hand

In placing the left hand on the club, the grip should run diagonally from the lower part of the palm, specifically right on the thickest crease in your palm, known as the

Jack Nicklaus's left hand.

Mickey Wright's left hand, partly in the fingers.

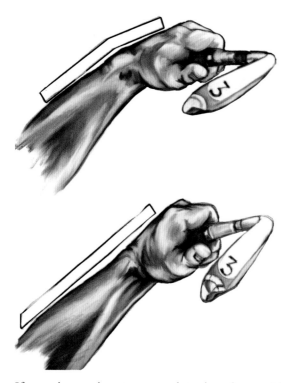

If one takes up the grip too much in the palm or with the thumb straight down the club, at the top of the swing the hand and thumb will likely not be in position to support the weight of the club and the stress of the transition. Hence, the club should be placed diagonally in the hand, with the thumb on the side of the shaft.

Line of Heart, across the top joint of your middle two fingers and lay on the middle joint of your index finger. Then the thumb is folded over and placed just to the right of the center of the club. The V formed by the thumb and index finger should point toward the right shoulder. If yours points toward your chin or right eye, keep turning it clockwise until it approximates the greats.

The placement of the left hand has a very distinct purpose. The left hand provides the stability in the strike but the full range of motion should never be compromised. The

Bobby Jones's perfect left hand placement.

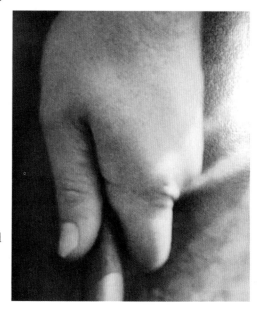

tendency is to take up the grip completely in the palm, but this is disastrous, as the player will lose some range of motion in the wrist and security of the club at the top of the swing.

Holding the club too much in the fingers is the better mistake, as at least one's mobility in the cocking and uncocking of the wrists will not be hindered. However, not enough of the left hand touches the club, so the tendency is to grip too tightly. The combination of a tight grip without enough connection points to the club will not support the blow of impact consistently.

The blend of having the club partly in the palm and partly in the fingers maintains control with the greatest amount of freedom and instinctively the right amount of pressure.

The placement of the thumb—not on top of the club, but just to the right of center—serves two very important purposes.

Because the plane of the swing is inclined, if the thumb were placed on the top of the club at address, at the end of the backswing the thumb's relative position would be on the left side of the club, where it is less likely to support its weight without increased tension. As a result, the pressure of the transition from backswing to downswing will have a tendency to limit the range of mobility in the hands. This will rob the player of a deeper set in the wrists, which is so important to accumulating power and will be discussed much later in this book in greater detail. At the top of the backswing it is better to have the left thumb underneath the shaft, where it is in a position to support the weight of the club. This is best done by having the thumb to the right of center at address.

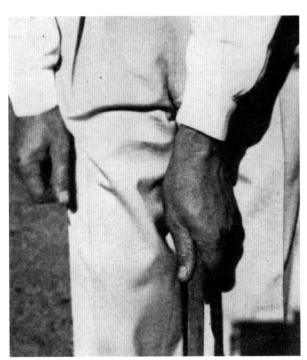

Byron Nelson's perfect left hand placement.

Ben Hogan's cupped compensation.

Ben Hogan overcame this problem by rolling his forearms and cupping his left wrist in an exaggerated way so that his left thumb was under the shaft at the top of the swing—in effect making his grip strong at the top, whereas it had previously been weak at the bottom.

Lastly, against the force of impact, having one's left thumb on the side of the club allows one a brace to push against and offset the collision of club and ball, providing stability at the swing's most violent point.

Nobody did this more obviously and stated it more clearly than Byron Nelson, who, in describing the position of the left thumb on the club in his book *Winning Golf* said, "the thumb of the left hand is closed on the shaft, a quarter of the way around." Thus a position many of the greatest players of all time found through trial and error was the best way to put their left hand on the club.

The Right Hand

Though the placement of the right hand is less complicated than that of the left, it is nonetheless the source of a great deal of confusion. There are remarkable players with all manner of styles when it comes to linking their hands together, and even a few who didn't at all. That choice has been entirely a personal preference and arrived at by experimentation.

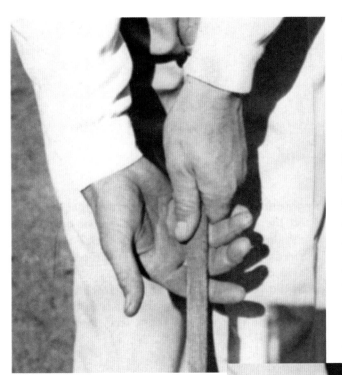

The club should run from the base of the top joint of the little finger, diagonally across the ring and middle fingers and rest on the middle joint of the index finger. The thumb should be placed on the left side of the club. This grip is illustrated by Byron Nelson, who used it to win eleven straight PGA Tour events and establish the lowest Sunday scoring average in history.

Ten-finger grip, interlocking grip, mesh grip, baseball grip, overlapping grip, and double overlapping grip.

Jones's hands perfectly placed on the club.

Jack Nicklaus

Majors have been won by players using every conceivable style of grip: overlapping, double overlapping, interlocking, a combination of interlocking and overlapping known as "mesh," ten-finger, and even baseball (where the left thumb is wrapped around the club).

There is little commonality in the way the best players have linked their hands together. However, *where* the right hand should be placed on the club is a matter of great importance, and many of the best players of all time have much in common in this regard.

The club should be entirely in the fingers of the right hand, running diagonally from the base of the little finger where it meets the palm, across the middle two fingers just below the palm and resting on the middle joint of the index finger. Then the right hand folds over the left hand, with the left thumb fitting snugly into the lifeline of the right palm. The right thumb rests not on top of the club but on the left side

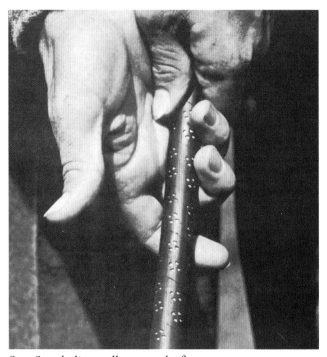

Sam Snead, diagonally across the fingers.

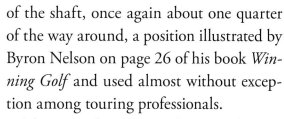

of the shaft, once again about one quarter of the way around, a position illustrated by Byron Nelson on page 26 of his book *Winning Golf* and used almost without exception among touring professionals.

The V, or line, as Mickey Wright preferred to call it, formed by the pressing together of the middle joint of the thumb to the side of the index finger will point to the right shoulder.

Many have advocated that this V should point to the chin or to the right side of the face, a position that is referred to as "weak." Besides the need for many manipulations to square the club from this position, a weak right-hand grip

MICKEY WRIGHT PUT THE CLUB diagonally across the fingers of her right hand until the club rested on the middle joint of her index finger and then put her thumb on the side of the grip, with the V's of both hands pointing toward her right shoulder, just as Lee Trevino did. This grip allowed Trevino to put the club in a "brink of disaster" position, discussed later in the book.

At impact the hands are in front of their address position, necessitating a strong grip to square the face.

puts the right arm above the left at address and can easily lead to an excessively open position of the shoulders in the setup. To be sure, there are examples of players who used this weak setting of the right hand with great success, but the majority of the best players throughout history have used a considerably stronger positioning of the right hand.

As stated earlier, the hands at impact are in front of where they were at address, and the stronger grip offsets the opening of the club as it is pushed forward coming into the ball.

Besides being the most efficient way to bring the club to square at impact, the placement of the right and left hands in the manner illustrated by these great players puts the arms and the hands in the proper alignment to take the club away without need of manipulation—a point I will magnify in later chapters.

Whether one chooses to interlock the little finger of the right hand around the index finger of the left or to overlap it in the small gap between the index and middle finger of the left hand, or perhaps to have all ten fingers on the club; whether one decides to have their fingers somewhat spread out on the grip as Ben Hogan and Mickey Wright did, or close together ("united") as Jack Nicklaus and Tom Watson did, doesn't matter anywhere near as much as where one puts the club in their hands and fingers and how they are angled on the club.

Ask the top 100 players of all time—or the top 100 teachers of today—what

From 1996 to 2002 when Tiger was most dominant in major championships, he used a grip where the V's pointed to his right shoulder.

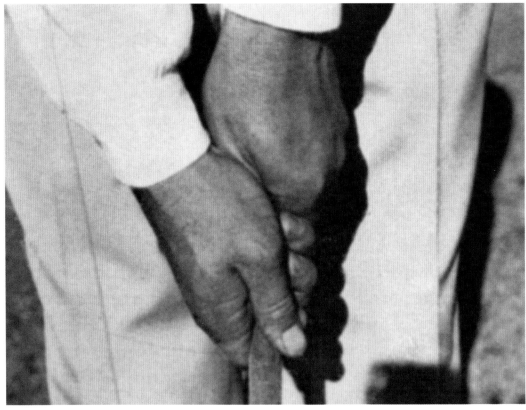

Byron Nelson's grip

Grip Pressure

There is a saying in martial arts that slow is smooth and smooth is fast. This is applicable to all sports. After six less-than-spectacular seasons with the Brooklyn/Los Angeles Dodgers, in 1961 Sandy Koufax was told by his backup catcher, Norm Sherry, that he could solve his problems by throwing the ball easier. From that point on Koufax said he tried to see how easy he could throw hard. Famed football coach Bill Walsh, notable for producing great quarterbacks, would stand behind young prospects and remind them to throw "easier," which made their passes more accurate and easier to catch and, in a counterintuitive way, increased speed. What do these stories have to do with grip pressure? Everything. Speed comes from relaxation and relaxation comes from practice, so practice your grip as described here. Train slow, train right, and if your hands are on the club properly you will instinctively have the right grip pressure to swing "easy."

is the most important position in golf, and to a man or woman they will say *impact*. But a proper impact cannot happen unless you have a proper grip. Put the club in your hands the way the best players of all time have, the way they are shown here, and if you still have a fault in your game you can look for it elsewhere.

Growing up in Texas, surrounded by Ben Hogan disciples, every strong grip I saw, with the V's of both hands pointing to the right shoulder, I saw as a compensation the player would have to make up for and a snap hook waiting to happen. As I progressed through college and onto the PGA Tour I noticed, more and more, that strong grips were the norm and indeed in looking back at the greatest players to have ever played this game, most of them, like Tom Watson, Henry Picard, Walter Hagen, Billy Casper, Arnold Palmer, and so many others, had used this grip.

The Setup

The greatest major champion of all time, Jack Nicklaus, was considered a slow player. He attributed that reputation to the amount of time he took to ensure he was properly set up to the ball. Nicklaus referred to the setup as "the single most important maneuver in golf."

Preparing himself to make a swing, Nicklaus completed a series of steps designed to prime every muscle, wake every joint, call to attention every part of the body, while still making sure he was relaxed enough to move freely. He positioned his feet, shoulders, club, and ball in such a way as to facilitate the proper path back and through for the desired shot.

Along with the proper grip, a sound setup gives you the best chance to play to your ability, to squeeze every ounce of speed and mobility out of your frame. And like the grip, the setup is a part of the game where the player has complete control —where a beginner can be as good as the best who ever played.

Width of Stance

From Ben Hogan to Tiger Woods, with few exceptions and within a very narrow range, the best players have set up with their driver so that lines traced down from the outside of their shoulders would come to a spot just inside their feet. Having their feet slightly wider than shoulder width apart gave them the freedom to move into their right side on the backswing while turning their hips so that they could brace on the inside of the right heel. This brace is then used to support the move in transition from backswing to downswing.

Tiger Woods and Ben Hogan addressed
the ball with the longer clubs so that a line
drawn straight down from the outside of
their shoulders would come to a spot just
inside their feet.

Within the range of stances from the narrowest—Bobby Jones—to the widest —Walter Hagen—the greats all found a base that allowed them to turn and move laterally in both directions.

Of course as the clubs got shorter, the stance got narrower, until with the shortest of irons, the feet were a few inches inside the shoulders.

The distance that you place one foot from the other in taking your stance will determine how well and to what degree you can both turn and transfer your weight on your backswing and through swing.

If your stance is too narrow, you will likely not have enough lateral shift to the right to keep the club low enough to have the proper width in your backswing.

Jack Nicklaus demonstrates how, as the clubs get shorter, the stance gets narrower.

Walter Hagen had the widest stance among the game's elite.

THE IDEAL STANCE FACILITATES the right amount of mobility, while providing the right amount of stability with the added benefit of allowing the player to move a little off the ball without tipping over to the outside of his back foot. This slight move off the ball sets the club on a low and wide path that helps create the widest possible arc, which helps create speed. The lower one's center of gravity, or wider the stance, the stronger one is, the higher one's center of gravity or narrower the stance, the faster one will be able to move, this right width stance provides the perfect blend of the two.

Bobby Jones's stance was notable for how narrow it was.

Jack Nicklaus with the ideal stance width.

You will have enough turn but because your base is not wide enough to support the turn you run the risk of your weight buckling to the outside of your right foot. That will cause you to lose the all-important brace in the right leg that allows you to maintain stability and generate power.

If your stance is too wide, you will struggle to move both your upper and lower body far enough back to establish a brace to properly begin the downswing. Conversely, if

Width of Stance

If one's stance is too narrow, a host of problems can occur. The club will likely cut to the inside abruptly, robbing the swing of width. Also, the golfer is likely to overturn the hips with too much weight remaining on the left and or causing the weight to buckle to the outside of the right foot, robbing them of the all-important brace of the right foot and leg.

Mickey Wright, set up perfectly.

Gary Player always started his swing by kicking the right knee to the target.

you do manage to get into your right side or set a brace by moving well off of the ball, you will struggle moving your weight toward the target.

Bobby Jones and Walter Hagen gave us the outer reaches of what is possible to do with any consistency, but among the best players in the history of this game their stances were idiosyncratic. Ben Hogan, Tiger Woods, Jack Nicklaus, Gary Player, Byron Nelson, Peter Thomson, and scores of others chose a stance width that was in between these two extremes.

The Right Knee

Of the many differences between professionals and amateurs and even between the best professionals and those of lesser skill, a player's success is largely related to how well the lower body is used on the downswing. This determines in what order, and in what manner, the parts of the body are used in delivering the clubhead to the ball. Proper lower-body movement depends in large part on the trigger motion of the right knee to begin the takeaway. Think of this part of the body as a starting block for a sprinter.

Almost every great player kicked the right knee in to start the swing. Some, such as Gary Player and Mickey Wright, did it in a more pronounced fashion than others, but this kicking in of the right knee is

Mickey Wright inclined her right knee at address and kicked it in more to begin the swing.

Alex Morrison believed strongly in the braced right knee to begin the swing.

one of the most important aspects in initiating the correct sequence of many movements that follow.

In Jack Nicklaus's *Golf My Way*, on page 96, he states that it was very helpful for him to set up with his right knee slightly inclined toward the target at address and to feel as if this brace were maintained in the backswing in order to get the proper leg action on the downswing. Where many others kicked the right knee in, Jack simply shifted his whole body slightly toward the target and then rebounded into his braced right knee to initiate the takeaway.

One of the more interesting changes to Ben Hogan's setup through the 1930s, '40s, and '50s, as he changed his swing to turn himself from a hooker to a fader, was the degree to which he inclined his right knee toward the target at address to use it as a trigger to begin the takeaway. This subtle change had profound effects with regard to the firing of his right leg in the downswing, specifically that he was able to "unweight" the right foot, which is to say his right heel came off the ground as the club approached hip high, and this contributed to the proper sequencing of the unwinding of his body and, I don't believe coincidentally, greater success with each passing decade.

Lee Trevino inclined his right knee at address and then kicked it in further to begin the swing.

That both Hogan and Nicklaus wrote about this often-overlooked key is no surprise, given that both great players are linked through a lineage of influences that traces its way back to Alex Morrison, (we already know) who wrote at great length about the need to start the swing with the right knee kicked in to initiate the motion of the swing.

Morrison believed that kicking the right knee in as little as two inches at address would compensate for a slight lateral shift—a corresponding two inches—off the ball without the weight tipping over to the outside of the right foot. The weight shift would lead to a low takeaway, giving width to the swing, while also giving the player a brace to start the downswing. All of this would be achieved by the simple act of feeling a little pressure on the inside part of the right foot to begin the backswing, something we see far too little of in professional golf today, where many look like their lower bodies have been carved in stone prior to initiating the takeaway.

Hogan in the 1930s.

Hogan in the '40s.

IT IS NO SECRET that Ben Hogan fought a hook early in his career and though he famously wrote that weakening his grip helped him stave of this hook, it is curious to me that as the decades passed and his swing evolved, he kicked his right knee more toward the target at address. I think this, as much as anything, helped him make the necessary moves to correct his hook. Specifically, it gave him a better brace to turn into on the backswing and from which to move into the downswing and allowed him to unweight his right foot (get the heel off the ground) so that he could use the pressure in that leg to rotate and straighten the left side, which is how an athlete achieves maximum velocity and in my opinion how Hogan got rid of his hook.

Hogan in the '50s.

Ball Position

Fixed or movable—that is the great debate in ball position. In other words, should you play every shot with every club from the same position in your stance, or should you move the ball forward incrementally as the clubs get longer? And what should the starting position be with the shortest club? Exact middle of the stance? Slightly forward of that (in line with the logo on your shirt)?

Jack Nicklaus, Ben Hogan, and Bobby Jones all believed in playing the ball from a consistent position forward in their stance, anywhere from the left instep, for Bobby Jones, to an inch or two inside the left heel, for Nicklaus and Hogan, for every club in the bag.

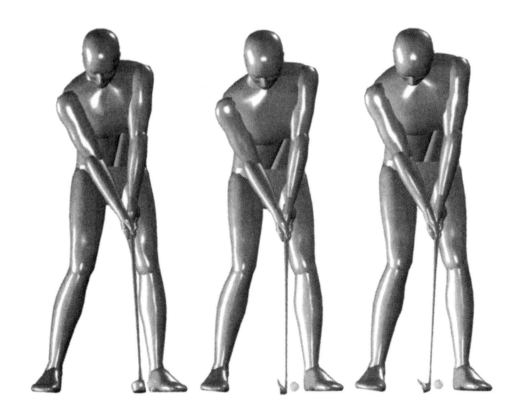

An average of Tour pros, proven in *Swing Like a Pro*, shows they vary their ball position very little.

Jack Nicklaus famously played the ball in the same place for every club.

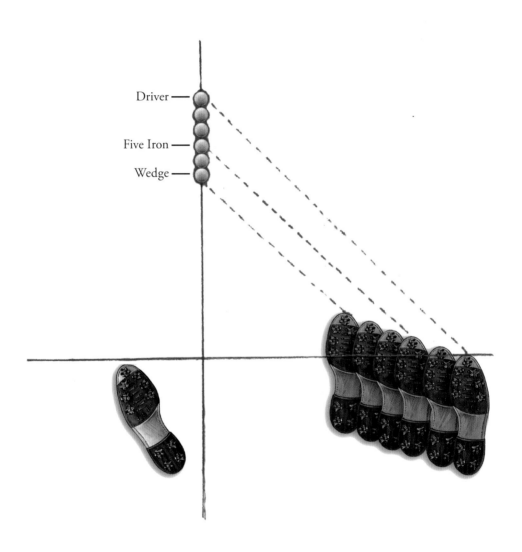

Both Jack Nicklaus and Ben Hogan preferred a static ball position.

Bobby Jones, like Nicklaus and Hogan, used the same ball position for every club.

Ralph Mann is a former world record holder in the 440 intermediate hurdles, a three time NCAA champion, a silver medalist in the 1972 Olympic Games and a member of the National Track and Field Hall of Fame and has a Ph.D. in biomechanics. He combined his love of sport with his understanding of motion and partnered with Fred Griffin to write *Swing Like a Pro*. With over a hundred Tour pros cooperating, Mann and Griffin used sensors and computers to capture their movements and arrived at many commonalities. One of them was how little ball position varied from player to player.

In *Bobby Jones on Golf,* the great amateur explained that in playing the ball forward, "that is, about on line with the instep of the left foot—at the top of the swing one will have the feeling that he can throw the whole weight and power of his body into the stroke, with the further advantage that the advanced position of the ball gives him more time to swing the clubhead into proper alignment."

Bobby Jones on Golf was published in 1931, the year after Jones won the Grand Slam. Sixty-seven years later, in 1998, came another book that used science to verify Jones's belief in the advantage of playing the ball forward in your stance. Dr. Ralph Mann was a hurdler who won the silver medal for the 400-meter hurdles in the 1972 Olympics and once held the world record for the 440-yard hurdles. Mann earned a Ph.D. in biomechanics from Washington State University. He combined his knowledge of sport with his expertise in science and movement to create models of performance for athletes. He cowrote the book *Swing Like a*

Tom Watson with his right knee pushed to the target.

Pro: The Breakthrough Scientific Method of Perfecting Your Golf Swing with PGA Professional Fred Griffin.

In a computer composite of more than 100 PGA and LPGA Tour players, Mann found that ball position "had an enormous influence on how your body reacts in your attempt to 'find' the ball with the club head. If the ball is positioned correctly, you can swing the club freely and soundly without having to make outlandish compensations with your body."

Some of the pros studied for the book varied their ball position by club, but only very slightly—less than three inches from the driver to the short irons. All positioned the ball forward of the middle of the stance even for the shortest clubs.

Positioning the ball forward in the stance sets a player behind the ball, creating the right amount of spine angle away from the target, which facilitates the turn and has so much to do with creating the right club path. Forward ball position also allows the player to move toward the target in the downswing without moving past the ball, which is, as you will see later, a commonality of the longest, straightest hitters in the history of golf.

When to Vary Position

While ball position might be more of a personal preference than most of the commonalities in this book, I think it is worth pointing out that Bobby Jones, Ben Hogan, and Jack Nicklaus, any one of which could reasonably be argued to be the greatest player of all time, all played the ball from a static position, well up in their stance. When one considers how much moving the ball around in the stance effects the angle of attack and the corresponding path of the club, they seem to have, through trial and error, eliminated many variables. There are, however, circumstances, where it is necessary to change ball position. For example, if your ball is in a divot you will need a steeper angle of attack and as such should move the ball back in your stance. If you are on a downslope, even after making the necessary adjustments in posture, you need to play the ball back in your stance. This is where experimentation is so important in the discovery of what compensations one must make for every conceivable situation, so by all means, try every ball position from every lie when practicing, because, other than tee shots, it is rare when one has a perfectly level lie on the course.

Posture

From the tallest major champion, George Archer, to one of the shortest, Ian Woosnam, there is understandably a remarkable difference in the amount of knee flex and spine tilt or bending from the waist. But this represents the extremes of not only what is possible, but in each of their cases, what was necessary.

At 6 feet 5 ½ inches tall, Archer played at a time—primarily the 1960s and '70s—when longer clubs of an acceptable weight and specification would have been very difficult to find, if not impossible. He made the necessary adjustments with his address position by bending over acutely and having a lot of knee flex. Woosnam, barely 5 feet 5 inches, stood almost straight up to the ball with very little spine tilt or bend in the knees.

Most of the greatest players, however, had much in common in their posture. Knee flex ranged from a little (Sam Snead) to a little more (Arnold Palmer), but in general, their legs were flexed so that if a line were extended downward from the top of the knees it would intersect with the balls of their feet.

The rest of the inclination that must be made to properly sole the club (where the bottom of the club rests on the ground, with only the slightest hint of the toe up in the air) was taken care of by the bend at the waist and the corresponding sticking out of the buttocks for balance.

It is the posture of the spine, however, that I would like to touch on in some detail. This is where I believe there has been a misunderstanding and there is some difference between the greatest players of all time and those of lesser accomplishment.

A CERTAIN DEGREE OF KNEE FLEX is necessary to prime the legs for action; in general if one is standing erect and looks down at the feet, the knees should be flexed until they are over the shoelaces. Sam Snead chose slightly less knee flex than this and Arnold Palmer slightly more, but among the best in this game there has been very little variance beyond these two "extremes." If the legs are locked or if they are excessively bent, one will not be able to move the lower body properly in the backswing and, it follows, the downswing.

Keeping the upper back straight and not rounded at address is a common point of modern instruction, and a glance up and down any range at a Tour event will show player after player with ramrod-straight backs. This might be aesthetically appealing, but I believe it's a case of overcorrection, also known as hypercorrection.

When trying to keep the upper part of the back straight, very often the lower part of the back becomes excessively concave. This tug of war to pull the spine straight creates far too much tension and makes it nearly impossible to get the fluidity that one seeks at the start of the backswing to say nothing of the truncating effect it has later in the swing.

If there is one area that has the most commonality among those who won the biggest events in golf, it is in the neutral or slightly concave position of the lower back and the *curved* position of the upper back at address. This is what they did.

The upper back is naturally curved to a small degree. When one inclines to the ball this allows the arms to hang naturally in front of the body and the hands to hold the club with the upper arms resting relaxed against the chest. There are numerous positive cumulative effects when this is done correctly and negative ones when done "hypercorrectly."

In transition from backswing to down-swing the upper back extends or expands as the body temporarily moves in two directions at once. When one's shoulders are curved at address—or drawn in toward the center of the body—they will be relaxed much like a pitcher's would be as he begins his throwing motion. It is this movement from a relaxed position to the expansion in transition that is the essence of athleticism in a swing, or pitch, as it were.

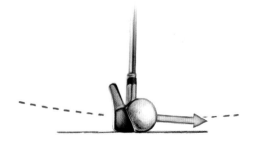

A properly soled club allows for a slight toe-down bend at impact.

If one starts from a position where the upper back is rigidly straight and the lower back is excessively concave, they are in a sense starting from the position they should be in when they begin the downswing and will lose the benefit of the expanding of the chest at the right time. That benefit being the continuing accumulation of power and the fluidity that comes from the proper sequence.

Besides the negative effect that this position has when changing directions in the swing, there is of course the tension that is required to maintain this erect posture that can only impede every athletic impulse. *You need to move laterally, rotationally, and vertically in the golf swing* to maximize power and none of these movements is accomplished best when a lot of tension is present.

It would have occurred to all of these great players at some time to try to hit a shot

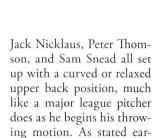

Jack Nicklaus, Peter Thomson, and Sam Snead all set up with a curved or relaxed upper back position, much like a major league pitcher does as he begins his throwing motion. As stated earlier, speed, though it comes from many things, such as efficiency of motion, is facilitated by relaxation and the greatest players of all time arrived at this relaxed position of the back instinctively. This allowed their arms to hang in the proper position, relaxed against their chest, so they could move into the backswing with little tension, which gave greater length to their swings and gave them room to expand their chests in the transition from backswing to downswing.

Charles Schwartzel

**WHAT CAN TODAY'S PLAY-
ERS LEARN FROM JACK NICK-
LAUS,** whose major wins spanned twenty-
four years, more than any other player in
history? A great deal, not least of which is
that they set up with too much tension present, evidenced by the almost rigidly straight
posture of their backs at address compared to
Jack's. Tense muscles will work against the
direction one is trying to move, complicating
every part of the swing thereafter and making one more susceptible to injury.

Adam Scott

THE PERFECT POSTURE OF DAVE THOMAS

In 1982 during the Open Championship at Royal Troon, I had dinner one night with Jack Nicklaus along with my college golf teammate Paul Thomas. At one point, I asked Jack who he thought was the best driver ever. He pointed to Paul and said, "His father, Dave." Dave Thomas, from Wales, lost the 1959 Open Championship in a playoff to Peter Thomson and the 1966 Open Championship by one to Jack Nicklaus and played on four Ryder Cups for Great Britain. Here he is at address, with a curved upper back, looking almost identical to every great player mentioned.

or two with a straight upper back and that thought would have been abandoned just as quickly for the contrived feel and inefficient results. I imagine if they would have had somebody they trusted standing close by insisting on this rigid position they would've been able to make it work in time, but never as well.

The Hall of Fame is full of those who would be guilty of slumping in today's hypercorrect world of "perfect" posture, but in this case, a little less exact is perfect.

Mariano Rivera, who had both longevity and consistency as one of the most dominant relievers in history, begins the pitching motion with a curved upper back and then his chest expands in the transition. He went from relaxed to a fluid delivery, the essence of athleticism, in accumulating and delivering power.

Look at the difference between Tiger Wood's posture when he was at his most dominant and when he was at his worst. The left picture was taken in the middle of his four consecutive majors. Notice the curved position of his back, versus the picture where he is keeping his back straight and there is much more tension present.

The Distance from the Ball

Perhaps because the greatest players have had sound grips and athletic and natural-looking postures there has been, at first glance, very little difference in how far they stood from the ball and how their arms hung at address. If one's hands are on the club properly it makes it hard to set up with them either too low or too high, perhaps causing one to be a corresponding too close or too far away from the ball. If one has good posture, it follows that the same is true.

Jack Nicklaus said that in taking his setup if an imaginary line were drawn from the top of his shoulders to the ball the left arm and club would dip slightly beneath this line and he liked to have a slight bend at the elbows. Almost every great player has had this look, where their hands hang just outside of a vertical line straight down from their shoulders, a look of freedom and comfort.

Jack Nicklaus stood fairly upright but neither crowded nor reached for the ball.

I will say though that I think history has favored those who stand closer to the ball and I don't think it is a coincidence.

Those who stretched a little to get to the ball were some of the great practicers of all time, men such as Ben Hogan, Gary Player, Lee Trevino, and the cultish figure of Canadian Moe Norman. Standing farther from the ball means that the club cuts more to the inside on the takeaway and comes into the ball on a shallower angle.

This shallower plane line means the clubhead will feel heavier mid-backswing and this sense of added weight can cause a responsive tensing of the hands, which one could argue disrupts the flow of the swing and requires more effort and practice to overcome. This is perhaps one of the reasons why flat swingers tend to be quicker and upright swings are more rhythmical. Sam Snead famously said that he could not watch Ben Hogan hit shots because of the flash of his tempo. Arnold Palmer, who similarly stood a long way from the ball, also had a very fast tempo, as did Moe Norman.

Moreover, to the degree that the angle of the club is shallower as it approaches the ball, all things being equal, the path or the movement of the sweetspot will be a corresponding amount more in-to-out or to the right of the target until the low point in the swing. The flatter or shallower the plane angle, again, all things being equal, the more hitting down or up on the ball will affect its path and hence the more important ball position becomes and the more precise a player has to be, which means there is a greater margin for error.

Bobby Jones stood fairly close to the ball, much like Byron Nelson.

Mickey Wright

In Sam Snead's book, *How to Play Golf,* on page 107, he says, "A stance too far away (from the ball) flattens the swinging arc, requiting extreme finesse to have the clubhead properly meet the ball." He goes on to say that standing closer to the ball gives one a more vertical arc and subsequently more accuracy. Byron Nelson famously said that it was almost impossible to stand too close to the ball.

Byron Nelson

CANADIAN MOE NORMAN, who has a cultish following in golf, was known to have been a great ball striker and like Arnold Palmer and Gary Player reached somewhat for the ball at address. This leads to a shallower swing plane, which makes the club feel heavier at mid-point in the backswing and downswing and leads to a shallower angle of attack. I believe this causes one to have a faster tempo and requires more maintenance than an upright swing.

Contrastingly, Byron Nelson said that one could not stand too close to the ball and in an effort to swing as upright as possible Jack Nicklaus assumed much the same look as Nelson at address. Which means that these two greats had much steeper backswings and downswings.

When the club is set on a steeper angle going back it feels light in the hands and one can maintain a lighter grip pressure throughout the swing. A lighter grip pressure means more relaxed arms and shoulders and as a result a longer swing with more rhythm and flow, which means one has more time to complete his or her turn.

When one stands closer to the ball the club approaches from a steeper angle, which means its path will have less curve relative to the ground, perhaps requiring less manipulation to square the face and less precise timing, to say nothing of the fact that it facilitates a higher ball flight.

Johnny Miller, legendary for laser-like irons and wide-margin wins.

Both Johnny Miller and Greg Norman stood close to the ball and swung on upright planes. Miller won twenty-five times on tour and for a period of time in the 1970s might have hit his irons as straight as anyone ever has. Norman, who played all over the world and won upward of a hundred tournaments, including twenty in the United States, was number one in the world for 331 weeks, second only to Tiger Woods since the world ranking's inception in 1986.

Greg Norman, statistically one of the longest and straightest drivers ever.

Given the benefits of standing a little closer to the ball, it is no surprise that fairly early in his career, once his swing became grooved, Byron Nelson said he could go three weeks without touching a club and it wouldn't affect him at all. Famously during his streak of eleven wins in a row in 1945 it was said that his pre-round warmups were never more than a half dozen or a dozen shots. As for Jack Nicklaus, in *Golf My Way,* on page 89, he said that "the ball is easier to hit when it is fairly close to you." And nobody hit it better than Jack.

Alignment

Perhaps one of the biggest misunderstandings about touring professionals is that they set up square to their target. This idea fits nicely with the railroad track analogy that is given, I'm sure out of convenience, to illustrate that the feet should be placed in such a manner that if a line were drawn across the toes it would be parallel to the target line, with the two imaginary lines extending off into the distance, resembling train tracks. If taken as true and applied to every club in the bag, you will likely be setting up to fail.

Thanks to the diagnostic equipment we have today we know that most professional golfers hit down on the ball with every club in the bag, if only slightly with the driver. I say "most" because there are a few who hit up on their drivers. As mentioned in the last chapter we know further that if the club is descending or going down, its path is going to the right of the target line.

This is why most professional golfers set up with their feet open, or to the left of their target line, offsetting with the alignment of their feet the path of the club. In Byron Nelson's book *Shape Your Swing the Modern Way,* on page 46, in bold type at the top of the page is the headline AIM AND ALIGNMENT: KEEP A SLIGHTLY OPEN STANCE. He goes on to say: "It makes it easier for the left side to move out of the way and the right side to come 'under' during the downswing."

Obviously more so with the shorter clubs and less so with the longer clubs, but with few exceptions this has held true throughout history.

Besides getting the swing on the correct path, this placement of the feet—open to the target line—gives the professional a head start to rotate on the downswing

Keeping the feet, hips, and shoulders slightly open, like most PGA Tour pros, helps generate more power.

and it is this rotation that is so important to the quality of the strike and to the speed of the swing. It is the speed of this rotation that helps the best players in the world create their lag, or the sharp angle between the left arm and the shaft of the club on the downswing.

If the feet are placed parallel to the target line, it is likely that you will know instinctively your path at impact, if not altered, will be well to the right of your target. You will also not be able to clear or rotate as quickly on the downswing

THIS RAILROAD TRACK ANALOGY has been put forth many times in golf's history and I believe sets most amateurs up to fail. Ralph Mann and Fred Griffen in the aforementioned book *Swing Like a Pro* found that Tour pros set up open for all clubs, if only slightly with the driver, and most of the greatest players have as well.

This illustration of Byron Nelson shows his open feet, hips, and shoulders.

as you otherwise would and again because your path will be to the right, you are further influenced to slow the rotation of your body, setting you up for the perfect combination of an over the top move to try to correct out of instinct what is offered up erroneously as a fundamental.

Of course this open alignment does not just apply to the feet. Most of the best players of all time had their shoulders slightly open, or left of, the intended target line. This allowed them, and will allow you, to "cheat" the downswing and rotate with all they had, which multiplies exponentially from the center of the body outward to the speed of the clubhead.

The faster one rotates, the easier it is to keep your arms tied to your body and vice versa. Think of the spinning figure skater, who elongates their limbs to slow down and draws them in to speed up. In golf this spinning, or rotation, draws the arms into the body as well, keeping the left one connected to the upper part of the torso in the early part of the downswing and the right one close to the side. This

Hitting Up on the Ball

If the club is moving down, or descending, when it hits the ball, then the club's center or sweetspot will be moving to the right, which is why Tour pros instinctively open their stances. A few players hit up on the ball with the driver, depending on flight preferences and swing speed, you might as well, in which case having a stance with the driver to the right or closed to the target might make sense for you. However, Bubba Watson, who is one of the few on Tour to hit up on his tee shots, and by quite a lot I might add, still sets up in an open stance (which is to the right for him, as he is a left handed golfer) and though he plays a massive cut shot, is still one of the most envied drivers in all of golf.

Tiger Woods, when winning four majors in a row, had a slightly open stance with his feet and his shoulders more open still. Maximum velocity comes from rotating, while straightening both the left side of body and legs through impact, and the greatest players of all time have found this is the best way to get a "head start" on that idea.

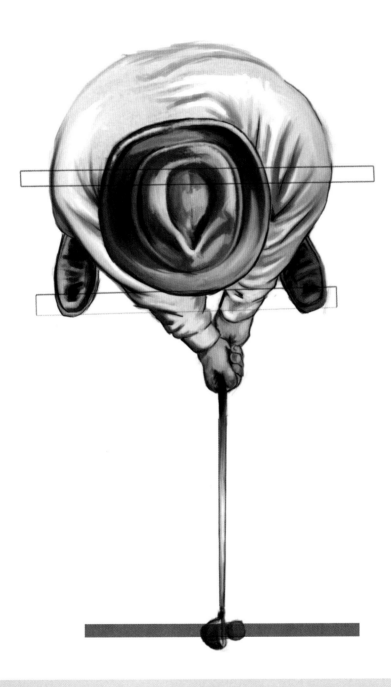

This illustration, based on page 46 in Byron Nelson's book *Shape Your Swing the Modern Way*, is meant to give the reader the idea of standing "slightly" open to the ball, which Byron argues allows for the right side to come "under" during the downswing and the left side to move out of the way.

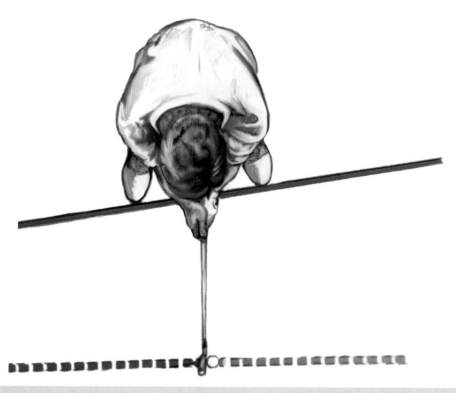

Jack Nicklaus, in a similar illustration to the overhead view of Byron Nelson, based on his book *Golf My Way* on page 85 shows a slightly open address position and says, "I do not, as so many golfers do, align parallel to the actual target line (dashed line)." Jack preferred a fade, and this slightly open stance facilitated that shot. The advantages of a fade are many, as it comes in higher and stops quicker, which on traditional back-to-front sloped greens means one has more uphill putts. The advantages of this over a career are illustrated by the successes of the two greatest faders of the ball in history, Ben Hogan and Jack Nicklaus.

rotation prevents one from losing the lag (the angle of the club and left arm) prematurely and it moves the bottom of the swing forward, delaying the hit, speeding up the swing, and providing proper club and ball contact. All of this, helped immeasurably by the simple act of opening up, if just slightly, the feet and the shoulders at address.

Bobby Jones, with a slightly open stance at address.

Spine Angle

I hesitated to touch on this element of the setup because if one has, like Jack Nicklaus did, taken extreme care to grip the club and address the ball properly, the spine will naturally be angled away from the target. Given that the ball is played forward, the right knee is kicked in and the right hand is lower on the club than the left, the right shoulder will quite obviously be lower than the left, which will orient the entire upper body slightly away from the target. Indeed the whole of the right side of the body will be slightly lower than the left, as it should be. The more the right knee is kicked in, as Gary Player and Cary Middlecoff did, the lower the right side will be.

What made me rethink excluding something that happened as consequence was the undeniable benefit of a low takeaway and great width to the backswing that is derived from setting up a proper angle in one's spine or having the whole right side lower than the left.

This low takeaway and width in the backswing allows one to get as much turn out of their shoulders as possible, and then to return the club on a sufficiently wide and shallow path.

In today's teaching, this position at address is known as the reverse K but long before there was a catchy name to describe what the best players looked like before they took the club away it was simply known as a proper setup.

Perfect spine angle.

Byron Nelson, Sam Snead, and Cary Middlecoff all set up in what today is known as a reverse K position at address, where the right side is lower than the left. This happens as a consequence of taking the proper grip, having the proper ball position, and kicking in the right knee at address. This causes the spine to be angled away from the target, if only slightly, and insures a low takeaway and gives width to the swing.

Ben Hogan, set up beautifully with the right side lower than the left, spine angled slightly away from the target, to ensure a low takeaway and proper weight transfer to the right in the early part of the backswing.

Bobby Jones, as he began his swing, turned his head to the right…and kept his chin pointed to a spot behind the ball until after impact.

The Position of the Head

Almost a hundred years ago, Alex Morrison in his book *A New Way to Better Golf* on page 49 stated that: "You must point your chin at a spot just back of the ball and keep it pointed there until well after the ball has been hit."

He went on to say that pointing one's chin behind the ball at address and throughout the swing was the most important single element in the correct swing and that it was not based on idiosyncrasies but on the anatomical structure of the human body.

Bobby Jones, having read Alex Morrison's teachings, said, "I am convinced that this is sound, for it places the head in a position where it will not tie up the rest of the body, either on the backswing or in the act of hitting the ball."

This positioning was patently visible in Bobby Jones as he turned his head to the right as he started his backswing, almost as a trigger, and he kept it pointed well behind the ball until after impact.

As did Byron Nelson, Ben Hogan, Sam Snead, and Jack Nicklaus. Jack turned

Jack Nicklaus, like so many greats before him, began his backswing by turning his head to the right and pointing his chin to a spot behind the ball, almost identical to the head position of Bobby Jones, the man whose record of thirteen majors he chased and ultimately passed. This position of the head allowed for a bigger turn of the upper body and kept passive in transition, if only for an instant, the right side of the body and allowed the proper sequencing of the downswing. This positioning of the head had its roots in the ideas of Alex Morrison, whose book *A New Way to Better Golf* expounded on this in great detail.

his head to the right because he said Snead did it and if it was good enough for Snead it was good enough for him.

Henry Picard, who won twenty-six times on Tour including the Masters and PGA Championship, was not only one of that era's best players, he was one of its best teachers. Ben Hogan's first book *Power Golf* was dedicated to Picard, who was taught the fundamentals of the swing plane by Alex Morrison and presumably passed them on to Hogan along with a suggestion to modify his grip to stave off a hook. I don't think it was any coincidence that both Snead and Hogan started their swings by turning their chin to the right.

Morrison's teachings hover in many great players but most extensively in Jack Nicklaus, who as a ten-year-old boy was taught the game by Jack Grout, who years before, learned much from Henry Picard.

Sam Snead, with his head turned to the right to begin the swing…and coming into the ball.

In the mid-1990s I saw sequence photos of Tiger Woods's golf swing and in them he had the almost identical head position of the great players. As the club approached waist high on the downswing, his chin was still pointed well behind the ball, the picture capturing perfectly a position common to the greatest players of all time. I remember thinking, there is no stopping this young man.

In turning the head to the right at address and pointing it to a spot just behind the ball, one makes more room for the shoulders to turn on the backswing, and in keeping it there as one begins the downswing, as most of the greats did, it promotes the desired shoulder movement in the transition.

The left side begins its target-ward move and stretches and the right shoulder, if only for a fraction of a second, is held back. In that fraction of a second the right shoulder drops, something I will discuss later in this book, setting the body up for an inside to down the line attack at the ball. This position of the head facilitates the stretch in the shoulders in transition and adds width to the downswing. Or to use the words of Jones once more, it puts the head in a position where it will not tie up the body on the downswing.

Ben Hogan turned his head to the right to begin his swing…and had his chin point to a spot behind the ball coming into the target.

Tiger Woods kept his head turned to the right, a position that foretold greatness.

Triggering the Swing

Unlike many other sports in which the athlete reacts to a ball in motion, the golfer must initiate all movement, and before the ball moves—before the club moves—the player must.

Almost without exception, going back to the earliest days of this game, the best professional golfers have written about the importance of the movement of the body that precedes the swing, to stave off tension. Some have waggled the club, like Ben Hogan, who famously wrote on the subject, while others like Bobby Jones and Lee Trevino took a few steps as they addressed the ball to kick-start their swings. Still others like Gary Player and Mickey Wright talked of using a forward press to initiate, as much by rebound, the beginning of the backswing. Jack Nicklaus and Sam Snead both used a combination of the forward press of their bodies, though it was more pronounced in Sam, and a turning of their heads to the right to serve as a preamble to their move away from the ball.

Perhaps one of the most ruinous trends in professional and amateur golf alike is the death of what Hogan called "the bridge" between the setup and the backswing. As the game's teaching has become more and more complex and microscopic in nature, players of all abilities have become frozen in thought over the ball and, it seems, have lost sight of the fact that the goal is to move in as big a circle as possible, as fast as possible, as smoothly as possible—and none of those three things can be accomplished as easily without being relaxed as the swing begins.

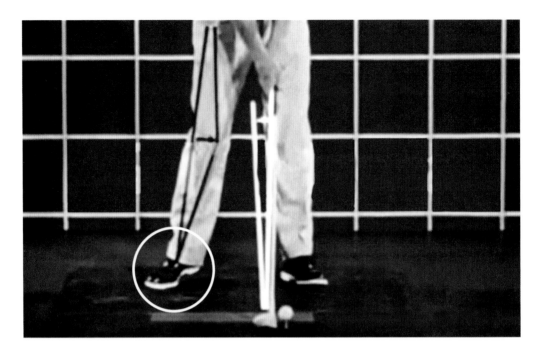

Sam Snead and Mickey Wright began their swings with an aggressive kick of the right knee to initiate, as if by rebound, movement in the opposite direction. Sam's triggering move was so obvious that his right heel came off the ground.

Gary Player and Lee Trevino set up with their right knees kicked in toward the target and then kicked them in even further to initiate movement in the opposite direction. This continuous flow of movement eliminates tension and the tendency to want to steer or guide the early part of the back-swing.

The Initial Move Away from the Ball

With what Jack Nicklaus called "the single most important maneuver in golf" accomplished, the first move away from the ball flows right out of, almost as a rebound from the waggle or forward press, and becomes an extension of the setup. This move set in motion a sequence that allowed the best to build, store, and deliver the full use of their power and to do so with incredible consistency.

As the right knee is inclined toward the target at address or kicked in during the forward press, the start of the backswing begins with the entire body moving back the distance that the right knee has been set toward the target. This move is slight but has conspicuous benefits for a number of reasons. To start with it keeps the hands quiet in the takeaway and this is important because to the degree the hands become active early on, the body becomes inactive and you want your body to move.

Jack Nicklaus

As the body moves laterally to the right, the feeling is of everything moving together, which means the hands will more likely stay relaxed and responsive until the critical moves necessary in the transition.

As the body moves laterally to the right it directs the club on a low path that is straight away from the ball, at least initially, which will help build width, which will produce a longer swing and give one more room and time to build power to say nothing of the proper rhythm.

To accomplish correctly, it requires one to feel as if the move is generated from the core or abdomen, with a hint of leaving the club behind, which engages the right muscles of the body and to the right degree, keeps those that will have power transferred to them later in the swing from ruining the sequence in the beginning.

All of these advantages from the simple act of shifting one's body, or weight if you wish, to the right no more than a few inches to begin the swing.

BEN HOGAN'S INITIAL MOVE OFF THE BALL showed a slight lateral shift to the right of a few inches because of the pressure in the right knee though his weight does not shift outside of the right foot. The trinity of the shoulders, arms, and hands has not changed and there is a hint of the clubhead being left behind. This sets Hogan up for a low and wide, powerful takeaway.

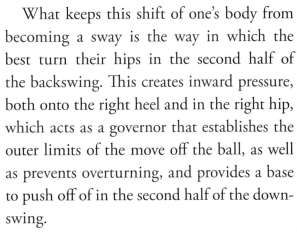

What keeps this shift of one's body from becoming a sway is the way in which the best turn their hips in the second half of the backswing. This creates inward pressure, both onto the right heel and in the right hip, which acts as a governor that establishes the outer limits of the move off the ball, as well as prevents overturning, and provides a base to push off of in the second half of the downswing.

Mickey Wright would practice with a golf ball under the outside part of her right foot to incline her foot toward the target, so important was the feeling of this brace to her building a proper backswing; and yet her head

Bobby Jones, like Ben Hogan, kept the shoulders, arms, and hands in the same relative position as they were in at address in the earliest part of the takeaway, ensuring a low and wide movement of the club away from the ball.

moved six to eight inches off the ball from its address position. She could do this because she never lost the stabilizing factor and the power source of the pressure on the inside part of her right heel and in the right hip. Ben Hogan called her swing the best he ever saw and I don't remember him saying she swayed off the ball.

Jack Nicklaus and Annika Sorenstam, as well as Peter Thomson (a golfing god to me who won five Open Championships from 1954–1965), not only moved their heads laterally in the backswing but they moved them up as well. This is a trait common among long drive champions like Jamie Sadlowski, who may be, given his size, the

JACK NICKLAUS, AFTER A SHIFT of his body to the left and a corresponding turning of his head to the right, moved the shoulders, arms, and hands low and wide off the ball (notice that there is no sign of Jack trying to set his wrists), completing in my opinion the best takeaway in the history of golf. Even though Jack famously talked of keeping his head still, in reality, his head moved slightly away from the target and slightly up in his backswing as his weight moved into his right side.

Sam Snead, with no sign of setting his wrists in his initial move off the ball—indeed there is a hint of him leaving the clubhead behind—sets the club on a low, wide takeaway. If this is done properly, as so many of the greats did, there is no need to ever have to think of the path of the club at any point on the backswing or downswing.

Mickey Wright maintains the trinity of the shoulders, arms, and hands to begin the backswing.

Tiger Woods, from 1997 to 2001, was the best driver of the ball in the world with the rarest combination in golf of great length and accuracy. During that time Tiger, as shown here, moved laterally off the ball as his weight crossed over to the inside part of his right leg and foot. Note there was no sign of him setting his wrists, indeed his takeaway thought, identical to that of Jack Nicklaus, who is statistically the longest and straightest driver in history, was to move the club as far away from the target as possible. This thought gives great width to the swing and causes the weight to shift to the right, both of which are critical to length and accuracy.

Mickey Wright, as demonstrated in her marvelous book *Play Golf the Wright Way,* used a drill of placing a golf ball under the outside of her right foot. This gave her a sense of pressure on the inside of her right foot and allowed her the freedom of moving off the ball in the initial part of the backswing without her weight moving to the outside of her foot.

Jamie Sadlowski, a two-time world long drive champion (2008 and 2009) at 5'11" and slight build, is a marvel of athleticism and may be, given his diminutive size relative to other long drive champions, pound for pound, inch for inch, the longest driver who has ever lived. Like Jack Nicklaus, who is unquestionably (with the best total driving number in history, which is a combination of length and accuracy) the longest and straightest driver ever, Jamie's head, during the takeaway, not only moved away from the target, it moved up as well.

most powerful golfer who has ever lived. The success and power of these players is no surprise because moving off and up from the ball requires an extension of both legs and since the downswing begins with a lowering of the body, this sets up the muscles first lengthening under tension and then shortening or contracting, something known as the stretch-shortening cycle, similar to the stretching of a rubber band.

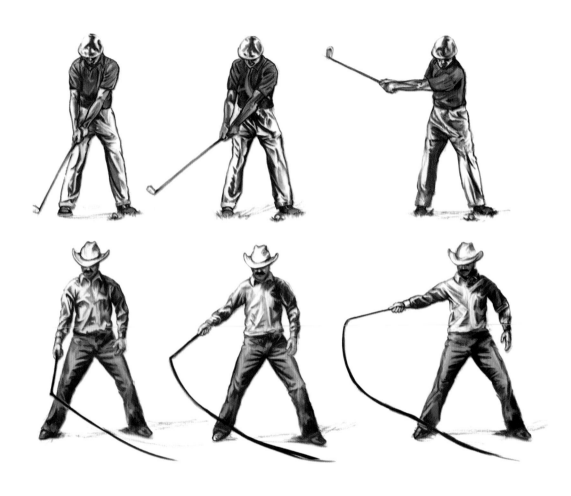

THE INITIAL MOVE AWAY FROM THE BALL can be likened, to some degree, to the initial move when one is cracking a whip, where the hand moves in the loading direction and precedes the tip of the whip. It is this feeling that one should have to execute the movement of the loading of the club and setting it on the right path.

Most people, if they think about this at all, only think about the stretch-shortening cycle in the second half of the downswing as it relates to squatting down and exploding through the golf ball. Jack, Annika, and Jamie Sadlowski came to this powerful up-move intuitively and use it to begin their backswings, a move that allows them to use gravity as they drop into their downswings, all of this accomplished by the end of the takeaway.

This shift off the ball has been called a one-piece takeaway (Jack Nicklaus called himself a "one piece" man) but every piece, or part, of the body is involved. The feet, legs, hips, hands, arms, and shoulders are all coordinated in what Jack

The Stretch Shortening Cycle: A Power Builder

The Stretch Shortening Cycle (SSC) is a phenomenon that is not fully understood, but there is no question as to the powerful benefits of stretching a muscle followed by the immediate shortening of that same muscle. This recruitment, or quick stretch, of a muscle makes it fire more powerfully. For example, one can jump higher when one first stretches up, as opposed to starting from a standstill, before one then squats down and springs up. It is thought that this changing of direction allows an athlete to tap into an energy that would have otherwise been dormant. This phenomenon to a lesser or greater degree happens at various points in the golf swing, which I point out going forward, in the recruitment of muscles, and the greatest players did things intuitively to bring this about.

Nicklaus called a "terribly forced ridiculously slow movement of the clubhead away from the ball." The clubhead will have moved three or four feet, the hands to a spot just past the right thigh, maybe only a foot or so, and the body just a few inches. The trinity of the shoulders, arms, and club will not have changed and if done correctly one need not worry about the path of the clubhead for the rest of the swing.

ANNIKA SORENSTAM, ON HER WAY to perhaps breaking every record in women's professional golf, until, like Bobby Jones and Byron Nelson, she retired at the height of her talents. Just like those two legends, Annika moved off the ball and kept intact her shoulders, arms, and hands as her weight and head moved well to her right with a hint of leaving the clubhead behind.

Annika Sorenstam was one of the longest, straightest drivers in LPGA history.

The Completion of the Backswing

With the pressure on the inside part of the right foot or heel, and the triangle of the shoulders, arms, and club intact, there is no more lateral shift to the right, and from here to the top of the swing the best strove for the most of two things: width and turn.

Only one man has won four professional majors in a row. Shortly after Tiger Woods accomplished this feat he wrote a book titled *How I Play Golf.* Between pages 162 and 163 of that book there is a foldout section with sequence photos of his swing beside the words: "The Swing That Won The Slam." On page 163 there is a back view of Tiger taking the club away from the ball with the bold type heading THINK "LONG AND WIDE" and one can clearly see that Tiger is trying to get his arms as far away from his body as possible as they approach hip high.

Patty Berg won fifteen professional majors, the most of any woman in history.

He writes that he tries to establish a very wide arc and that to do so, he extends the butt end of the shaft as far from his right hip as he possibly can, his shoulders turning to make it happen. One can clearly see that his right leg is angled toward the target a bit, even though he has obviously shifted his weight to the right. This is evidence that the weight is on the inside part of the right foot as he stretches into his backswing.

Jack Nicklaus similarly in his book *Golf My Way* on page 109 states that as his hands

approach hip high, "My left arm is extended as far as it will go from my body and ideally, the club and my left arm still form a straight line—no wrist hinging yet. My right arm, still passive, has moved well away from my side to allow full extension of the left arm, but my right elbow does not 'fly.' "

Greg Norman has been called one of the longest and straightest drivers in history and statistics bear this out. In his book *Shark Attack* on page 72 he states: "The farther you can extend that clubhead away from your body (while still maintaining good balance and timing) the longer you will hit the ball."

Sam Snead, Greg Norman, and Byron Nelson had the club as far away from the target as possible.

Jack Nicklaus, with his right arm well above the left at this stage of the swing, ensured a very wide and powerful windup on the backswing.

At this stage of the swing the best players have made no effort to set their wrists, which would cut their swing arcs appreciably, and unnecessarily rob them of the late loading of the wrists, nearer to the end of the backswing, in yet another stretch-shortening cycle of the muscles, albeit this one of the smaller muscles in the arms and hands.

As the left arm and club extend away from the target and the hands reach hip high, the right arm is above the left (if viewed from face on, the right arm is not obscured by the left) and has separated from the body. The right hand has pronated slightly (turned counterclockwise) and extended a bit (broken up toward the wrist), which puts the clubface in what has been called a shut position.

NOTICE THE POSITION OF THE RIGHT HAND for Jack Nicklaus, Arnold Palmer, and Sam Snead. At this point in the swing it is facing slightly down to the ground in what is known as a pronated position. This is contrary to the "toe up" principle or rotating clockwise of the right hand thought that is so often espoused as necessary to a correct backswing. As you will see, most athletic moves, in the loading process, have the right hand (for a right hander) facing slightly to the ground.

Jack Nicklaus, with what is called a "shut" position of the club.

Byron Nelson in an identical position to that of
Nicklaus with the right hand of the club.

The benefits of this shut position are immense as it keeps one from rolling the arms clockwise during the backswing—which you want to do during the transition (more on this move later)—but if you do it during the backswing you will likely be too open or laid off on the downswing, something Tour pros call "getting stuck," and you will need to flip the hands to square the clubhead.

Yet time and time again I read and hear it said that one should have the clubface in a "toe-up" or "square" position when the hands reach hip high. This is why "getting stuck" is a common refrain on Tour these days. We have been told that the right palm should open up or roll clockwise in the backswing. Imagine if a quarterback or a pitcher tried to throw a ball in this way, rolling the throwing arm and hand clockwise in the loading motion. They would loose the stretch-shortening cycle of the muscles in their hand and arm in the transition, lose power and accuracy, and never be heard from again. It is this slightly shut position of the clubface that one wants when the hands are hip high and nobody did this better than Jack Nicklaus and Byron Nelson.

Tom Brady

Nolan Ryan

Roger Federer

Brett Favre

WHEN LOOKING AT THE RIGHT HAND POSITION OF ALL OF THESE GREAT ATHLETES, one can see that in the loading motion the right palm faces the ground, in what is called a pronated position. This position of the right hand sets up a stretch shortening cycle (outlined earlier) in the transition from backswing to downswing, in the smaller muscles of the wrist and forearm that generate a great deal of power to say nothing of putting the whole right arm and hand on the proper path to deliver the club, or in the case of these athletes the ball or racket.

With the right arm on top and the right hand pronated and slightly extended at hip high, the right hip has begun to move rearward, and the right leg has begun to extend or straighten and it is on this point that I would like to talk about perhaps the single biggest difference between the greatest players of all time and far too many of today's Tour pros.

Somewhere in the 1980s it became fashionable to maintain a lot of flex in the right knee in the backswing, the idea I suppose being that one builds tension by squatting into the right leg and that squat resists the hips' movement which in turn allows one to build torque by turning the upper body against this resistance, like the loading of a spring we were told. The premise of this theory is so massively incorrect and its problems so numerous that for over thirty years it has almost completely divested the PGA and LPGA Tour players of their ability to build on the methods of a previous generation, not to mention their athleticism, rhythm, and health.

The coiled spring analogy that is offered up in this game to convince players to resist with the lower body could not be more wrong.

To start with, the muscles and the fascia of the body do not have the same properties of a coiled spring. Regardless of how much torque or axial tension one thinks they are creating with the resistance of the lower body, there is not enough spring-like effect or automatic release of energy to offset the corresponding loss of turn. This capital crime of expository commentary has been packaged and sold to amateur and professional alike and it is pure myth.

When one keeps a lot of flex in the right leg and resists with the lower body, the right hip will be closer to the target line and lower than desirable. This will impair

Ben Hogan and Sam Snead with their right legs straightened and weight loaded—a position you want to copy.

Jack Nicklaus made no attempt to resist with the lower body on the backswing.

Nor did Bobby Jones.

or eliminate the up-move—previously discussed—and can result in a potentially disastrous buildup of tension and stress in the entire body. This will, more than likely, result in the premature firing of the lower body, which can lead to something Tour pros call "getting stuck," which simply means the body has outraced the arms.

Moreover because the right hip is too far forward one can't fully load their weight into the right heel, a position almost every great player found to provide the perfect brace for the backswing.

When one keeps the flex in the right leg and resists with the lower body, the resistance shortens the hip turn and the amount that the torso and the shoulders turn, robbing the player of the powerful assets of time and space. Because the player doesn't have as much time or space to create speed, there becomes an urgency to the transition and a need for explosive power to compensate. This explosive transition not only robs a player of their rhythm but because it takes a lot of effort and tension to resist the turning of the lower body, the muscles in the legs, hips, and lower back can be stressed to their limit and then are asked to accelerate to their maximum, which is the perfect recipe to cause injury, especially to the lower back and hips.

Bobby Jones

When we hear players say they need to be more explosive, it's because they have lost the time and space to build power in their swings and they are trying to trade strength for speed.

If this theory of resisting with the lower body did in fact make one more powerful, then why doesn't every long drive champion employ this method? They are looking for every yard they can find and they turn their hips far more than is commonly (almost universally) prescribed, perhaps no one more perfectly than Jamie Sadlowski.

If this theory of resisting with the lower body did in fact make one a better golfer then why is it that almost every Hall of Fame player, man and woman alike, turned their hips far more than what is currently

Peter Thomson

Walter Hagen

Byron Nelson

taught or is fashionable? Indeed if they have anything in common, most of the best players of all time look plagiaristically identical in this position. To restrict

Jamie Sadlowski. If it were really true that resisting with the lower body made for a more powerful swing, then why don't long drive champions follow this axiom? Because, very simply, it is not true.

with the lower body is to say that all of these players didn't know what they were doing.

At the top of the backswing, with few exceptions, the best players have had their right leg extended and their hips fully turned such that their lower back or sacrum is closer to the target than it was at address. The left knee has broken in and points behind the ball and the left heel has risen off the ground with the longer clubs. This last point seems to invite much scorn, even in the increasingly scientific world of golf instruction, but none of us needs an NSF grant to see what is in plain view. How could it possibly be bad for the average golfer to raise his left heel when it was so important for the best golfers to do so?

The Transition

One could easily write an entire book about the little more than one foot that the club travels from the end of the backswing to the beginning of the downswing. This loading of the club happens in a fraction of a second and is often overlooked or mistaken and perhaps weakened in significance by the one-word name given to describe this critical area of the swing.

The importance of the transition is such that one can arrive at the top of the backswing looking like a pauper and a foot or so later become a legend, as well as the other way around. At the top of their swings, Miller Barber, Gay Brewer, Ray Floyd, Larry Nelson, Calvin Peete, and Jim Furyk look like an irreversible calamity about to happen and yet within this group of men, all of whom won at least ten times on Tour, are multiple major winners, Hall of Fame members, and, in Calvin Peete, statistically the straightest hitter who ever lived. The juxtaposition of their unorthodox-looking backswings to their downswings helps one understand the

Ray Floyd looked unorthodox at the top and an instant later is in perfect position.

importance of the transition. In more traditional-looking swings, however, the moves that the greatest players have made linking the backswing to the downswing are harder to discern.

The flip side of this are countless amateurs with outstanding top of the backswing positions who are endlessly frustrated by their lack of success. Without a good transition a player cannot achieve the combination of speed and accuracy common to the best players.

Arnold Palmer, in his transition from backswing to downswing, begins with the lower body and his left side moving toward the target, while the upper body is still turning back, creating a two-way stretch, which lowers the right shoulder and fully loads both wrists.

Gary Player, well into his transition, as the right side holds.

The upper-class of the game's elite, players such as Walter Hagen, Bobby Jones, Gene Sarazen, Sam Snead, Byron Nelson, Ben Hogan, Cary Middelcoff, Peter Thomson, Gary Player, Mickey Wright, Arnold Palmer, Jack Nicklaus, Billy Casper, Lee Trevino, Tom Watson, Annika Sorenstam, and Tiger Woods, to the degree that they were better than their peers, they beat them in that space between the backswing and the downswing, where power is accumulated and stored, to be delivered an instant later.

Sam Snead, with the best transition in the history of golf, arrived at the top of his swing with an almost straight right leg and massive hip and shoulder turn. From there he could move the left side of his body toward the target while keeping the right side passive. This kept his left hip lower than his right and gave him a definitive squat in the legs.

A look at the greatest transition in golf shows Sam Snead from behind and the left hip clearly lower than the right, not only at the top of the swing but also well into the downswing, which is so important to long straight drives and happens as a consequence. Also clearly visible here is the holding of the right side, resulting in the right knee kicking out in the direction it is pointed in at the top, resulting in his famous squat, to a lesser degree common in almost every great player.

Peter Thomson with the left hip lower than the right.

Tom Watson with the left hip lower than the right.

Having done most of what has been laid out in this book up to now, the above players began the downswing by moving laterally, shifting their lower body and their weight toward the target while still completing the windup of their upper bodies. Because most of these players had turned their hips as far around as they could comfortably go, as their weight began to move toward the target, their lower back or sacrum moved in that direction as well. This action inclines the left hip at an angle slightly lower than the right hip and puts pressure into the left foot. That pressure will be used an instant later to push off of and stretch the left side.

At this point the upper and lower body are moving in opposite directions, something Jack Nicklaus called the "two way stretch," but so much more is about to happen as a consequence of this stretch. As the body begins to rotate toward the target, the chest expands as the left arm gets stretched and the right shoulder drops and rotates externally or clockwise. The right knee, because of how it is pointed, say at two o'clock on the face of a watch, kicks out in that direction and the heel begins to come off the ground. As the left knee had a head start, the player looks to be squatting. This squat, most visible in Sam Snead, can be seen to some degree in almost every other great as well. This reversal of the lower body and the simultaneous stretch and expansion of the upper body is the essence of

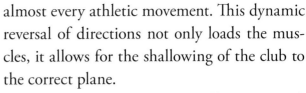

almost every athletic movement. This dynamic reversal of directions not only loads the muscles, it allows for the shallowing of the club to the correct plane.

In his book *How I Play Golf,* on page 34, Sam Snead said of this point in the swing that there "is a definite pull on the left shoulder and arm."

Because the wrists were never consciously set by most of these players in the backswing, they achieve maximum load right here in a stretch-shortening cycle that would have been eliminated if the wrists were actively set early in the backswing.

Tiger Woods and Sam Snead held the right side in transition, lowered the right shoulder and the right wrist fully loaded and turned slightly counterclockwise or pronated.

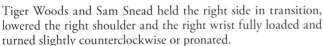

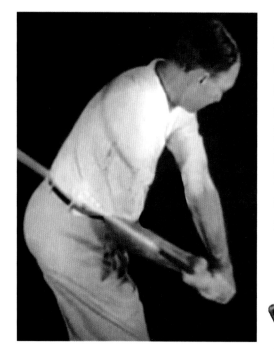

However, it is not just that the angle in the right wrist increases but how it increases. As the right wrist fully loads it has a hint of turning counterclockwise (pronates) and folds backward, something known as extension. As the right hand is turning counterclockwise and folding back on itself, the right elbow moves toward the right hip and the right arm moves as if one is losing an arm wrestling

BEN HOGAN in *Five Lessons* had illustrations showing what he believed to be his positions on the downswing, both in the transition and delivering the club to the ball. This middle illustration here is based on the photograph from *Life* magazine where he was posing for the illustration that made its way into that famous book. If one looks at the position of his right hand you can see that he is "posing" with it pointing toward the sky but in reality as one can see from the top high speed photo Hogan's right hand was nowhere near that position and was far more pronated or inclined toward the ground, which put the club in a position far different to the one he has illustrated at the bottom of this page. These pictures have misled advocates for years and have led to an epidemic of people "being stuck" on the downswing.

Dangers of Resisting with the Lower Body

If one resists with the lower body on the backswing, it puts the right knee and leg in a very stressed position, from which far too often the right knee kicks in at the beginning of the downswing. This robs one of the benefit of this move if used a fraction later. The kicking in of the right knee, or should I say the extension of the right knee and leg on the downswing, is a very powerful move and can only be used once, and once used, can not be used again. Hence why the squat in transition is so important. If one kicks the right knee in immediately to begin the downswing it also has the detrimental effect of raising the left hip above the right and causing a whole host of problems, not the least of which is too much spine tilt on the downswing.

Tiger's right elbow perfectly pointing to the right hip.

match. These movements create a two-way stretch of just the right arm.

If the right elbow moves toward the right hip and the right arm moves as if one is losing an arm wrestling match, without the right wrist turning counterclockwise, the clubface will be open and the shaft under the plane and in a very poor position to be delivered to the ball. This will require one to compensate, likely by stalling with the whole body in order to flip the hands to square the club.

This open position happens frequently, even on Tour, and probably has its roots in the inaccurate drawings in *Five Lessons* by Ben Hogan on page 95 and 99, showing the right elbow in front of the hip and the right forearm and hand turned clockwise, something Ben Hogan did not do in his actual swing, nor did most of the people in his stratosphere of accomplishment. The inaccuracies in these drawings are understandable given the speed of this movement. Regardless though, it is a mistake you do not want to make.

Jack Nicklaus, Tiger Woods, and Ben Hogan all had, to a lesser degree than Sam Snead, their version of the squat in transition. The right side has held in each to some degree as the left side moved away, keeping the left hip lower than the right, which helped save the all-important kick, or extension of the right leg and knee, until later in the swing.

This sequence of moves happens so smoothly and quickly and for the very best players, innately, that the transition frequently gets summed up as merely dropping the arms down to the side while transferring the weight to the forward foot, but it is vastly more complicated than that. Although many of these complications could be alleviated simply by turning more on the backswing.

In this era of minimal hip turn and excessive knee flex in the right leg, it is almost impossible to squat in transition because the right knee, if held in flex during the backswing, will want to kick toward the target in transition, which will prematurely raise the left hip, and the legs having already fired early in the downswing will stall and this will lead to a myriad of compensations.

When we watch the best players of this era and eras past and there is something we can't quite put our finger on that makes them look vastly superior to other players, it is usually because they own that conversionary space from backswing to downswing known as the transition.

Impact and the Finish

The aggregate effect of the "two way stretch" has lengthened the left side and loaded the right side, which is to say, cocked the right wrist in such a manner that the club has closed slightly in relation to the plane of the left arm, which sends a message to the body to turn with all its might. This slightly closed position of the clubface is what Lee Trevino referred to as "the brink of disaster move" that was so important to triggering his turn.

Because the right knee didn't initially kick toward the left knee it allowed the right elbow to drop to a position tending toward the front of the rib cage, with the right hand still in a position turned counterclockwise or pronated. The reason so many have struggled when trying to duplicate this right-elbow movement is because they didn't have the corresponding pronation of the right wrist, again perhaps owing to the confusion of the drawings in *Five Lessons*. From here to the finish the geniuses of this game were free to rotate as fast as they pleased without worry of being out of position.

The weight, or some would say pressure, has moved to the left foot, but not to the outside of the left foot, indeed Jack Nicklaus, whose teacher Jack Grout

Ben Hogan, delivering the club to the ball, far different than what was illustrated in *Five Lessons*.

Lee Trevino, in what he called his "brink of disaster" move.

Jack Nicklaus

Tom Watson

Ben Hogan. Notice the bowed left wrist and closed clubface.

stressed playing off the "insides of the feet," makes this point emphatically. As the weight didn't move to the outside of the left foot, the left hip, as it rotated up and back, elongating the left side, which brings the hands to a position about hip high in the swing, and it is here that all hell breaks lose.

The right knee, hip, and ankle extend, which brings the right heel considerably off the ground. The left side continues to extend and the body rotates as if it were a revolving door, as opposed to a door on hinges. In addition the left wrist flattens or, in the case of a weaker grip, bows. This combination of movements causes the right side to bend laterally, bringing the right shoulder closer to the

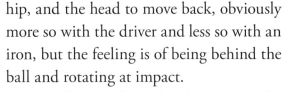

hip, and the head to move back, obviously more so with the driver and less so with an iron, but the feeling is of being behind the ball and rotating at impact.

The left side, from the shoulder to the foot, is fully rotated and stretched, and the left arm and club form a line that is only slightly in front of the ball. The right arm has not fully released and the right wrist is still in extension or bent slightly back. An instant later after the ball is gone the right arm releases completely. The greatest major champion, Jack Nicklaus, has stated that even though the whole unit of the arms and club

Bobby Jones, Byron Nelson, and Jack Nicklaus all extended and rotated their left sides through impact allowing the right side to bend and move "under" as the feeling is known to these greats as the club released. It is worth pointing out that Byron Nelson, who was said to have a dip with his legs at impact, clearly is elongating his left side as it rotates and his legendary dip came primarily after impact.

Perfection.

is forced to swing to the left, the feeling is of swinging out toward the target or "out and up," not "over and around." Tiger Woods continues this thought on page 155 in his book when he says in bold print, "The feeling here is one of throwing the clubhead down the line with my right hand." This extension of the club on the follow-through carries these great players to a fully extended finish, but the speed of the rotation very often has them firing and falling backwards, belying the myth, and hence the necessity, of "sticking the finish."

Swinging Down the Line

WITH SO MUCH IN VOGUE TALK OF "SWINGING LEFT" after impact, something that quite naturally happens as a consequence of one standing to the side of the ball, it's worth noting that the greatest players of all time felt as if the club went down the line after impact. Similarly, players are encouraged to finish in balance when hitting a big drive, and that nothing should be done at the expense of balance. Yet almost every great player fired and fell back on the finish of their swing. They were, once the initial move toward the target in transition was completed, rotating and extending so beautifully and fully that the momentum at the finish required them to pull their left foot back toward their right to keep from falling over.

Jack Nicklaus firing and falling back.

Harry Vardon, who was born in 1870, won seven majors and finished second in the U.S. Open when he was fifty years old. Decades later his impact position hasn't been improved upon.

Byron Nelson, who some say played the greatest golf ever, won eleven straight Tour events in 1945.

Jack Nicklaus, decades after Harry Vardon, with much the same look.

Sam Snead. Nobody in the history of golf did all of the things in this book more thoroughly and beautifully.

Summary

I f it is true that longevity sanctifies, that the truest test of anything is time, be it a government, a relationship, an idea or in this case the form of a few golfers, then we should never try to escape our past. In fact to confront what has endured is a transaction in knowledge. Yet I have seen so much of what has succeeded and endured in this game dismissed as idiosyncratic, such as Sam Snead's squat or Jack Nicklaus's flying right arm or Arnold Palmer's shut clubface.

I have seen much in this game misunderstood and offered up for its aesthetic appeal as well. Beautiful but wrong, like a geocentric model of the universe centuries ago, because until recently there hasn't been the equivalent of the telescope to the "stars," but now high-speed cameras and three-dimensional analysis have allowed us to connect all of the dots.

The past giants of this game cast long shadows but it's as if the shadows are unseen to us, such is the diversity of technical opinion offered up and argued about in this game today. Which brings to mind a quote by the thirteenth-century Persian Poet Rumi, who said, "Maybe you are searching among the branches, for what only appears in the roots." When asked about this book, I have always said it was an instructional book but it was not I who was doing the instructing but rather the greatest players of all time.

Acknowledgments

To the men and women whose golf swings and ideas have never ceased to inspire and entertain me: Harry Vardon, Macdonald Smith, Alex Morrison, Henry Picard, Bobby Jones, Sam Snead, Byron Nelson, Ben Hogan, Arnold Palmer, Tom Watson, Lee Trevino, Tiger Woods, Mickey Wright, Louise Suggs, Patty Berg, Babe Zaharias, and Jack Nicklaus. This book would not have been possible without everything they have contributed to golf.

To my friends who revealed much that had always been true but was unknown to me until they explained it: Fred Griffen, Ralph Mann, Jeff Martin, Lucas Wald, Jack Harden Sr., Rives McBee, and Brian Henniger.

I am indebted to everyone at the Golf Channel. They not only gave me the opportunity to stay in the beautiful world of golf, but allowed me to express my opinions on this great game and the fascinating and talented people in it. The people at the Golf Channel are not only my colleagues, they are my friends.

I also want to thank Brian Lewis and Mike Beckerich at Classics of Golf. They are as dedicated as I am to this great game. I can't thank them enough for their belief in me as a writer. This book would not have been possible without them. They allowed this book to be mine, and it is more powerful because of that. And to the many people at Simon & Schuster who have helped: my gratitude is never ending.

To Mike Short, whose friendship and love of old golf books have been a constant source of comfort.

To Jack Harden, whose passion in talking about the golf swing reminds me of Ahab pursuing the white whale and whose friendship knows no boundaries.

And finally, to my family. There is one thing I love more than golf—and it will always be you.

Brandel Chamblee joined Golf Channel in 2004 and currently serves as a studio analyst for *Golf Central* as well as an analyst for the network's "Live From" programming, airing on-site from the game's biggest events. He also writes for GolfChannel.com and for years wrote the back inside cover feature for *GOLF* magazine.

Chamblee has earned a reputation for being one of the most intellectual, accurate, insightful, and well-researched personalities on Golf Channel. He is known for his keen knowledge of the golf swing and the history of the game. His insights and opinions on the game's biggest stars are why the *New York Times* says he is "Golf Channel's resident scholar and critic…has an artist's way with words."

A PGA Tour winner, Chamblee enjoyed a fifteen-year professional playing career that included more than $4 million in earnings. His career highlights include victories at the 1998 Greater Vancouver Open on the PGA Tour and the 1990 Ben Hogan New England Classic on the Web.com Tour. He also shared the first-round lead at the Masters in 1999 and finished within the top 100 on the PGA Tour money list for seven consecutive years.

Photo Credits